Hello!
You've probably had an idea and said to yourself...

"That would make a great book"

In your head it's written, a publisher has snapped it up, you're about to have your book launch debut... it all sounds pretty awesome doesn't it?

However, in reality there are many steps before you reach such dizzying heights of success. This book is here to help you. It is part:

- ☐ **Overview** - brief industry overview and bite size advice
- ☐ **Check list** - tick off what aligns with you
- ☐ **Journal** - a starting point for ideas, thoughts and doodles

It will give you enough information to understand and talk with those involved in the publishing industry. It's full of insights and will steer you in the right direction. It also shares some insights that aren't obvious about the reality of being an author.

So, **are you ready to be an author?** Let's find out...

Published by Share Your Story
Share Your Story
PO Box 5447
Alexandra Hills QLD 4161
Printed by Ingram Sparks

First published in Australia 2021
This edition published in 2021
Copyright © Trish Donald 2021
Author and Illustrator Trish Donald
Cover design by Working Type Studio

The right of Trish Donald to be identified as the Author and Illustrator of the Work has been asserted in accordance with the Copyright, Designs and Patents Act 1988.

All rights reserved. No part of this publication may be reproduced, stored in a retrieval system, or transmitted, in any form or by any means without the prior written permission of the publisher, nor be otherwise circulated in any form of binding or cover other than that in which it is published and without a similar condition being imposed on the subsequent purchaser.

Trish Donald
So, You Wanna Be An Author?
ISBN: 978-0-6487732-2-1

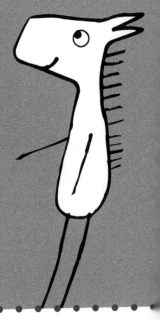

This book belongs to:

Publishers

There are many ways to be published

Who is the right fit for you?

Publishers have specific books that they want to publish. Some only publish picture books, or self-help books, while others publish a variety such as chapter books for kids, young adult literature and novels for adult audiences. They vary in size from the large traditional publishers that most people have heard of such as Penguin and Scholastic, to small independent niche publishers. Understanding what publishers are looking for is the way to navigate the industry and find a good fit for you and your book.

☐ Traditional publishing

To be traditionally published means that a publishing company offers a contract to an author and in doing so owns the rights to the story. The publisher is responsible for everything that's involved in taking a manuscript and turning it into a book. This includes things such as editing, finding an illustrator (if the book requires one), printing, advertising, distribution to retailers and all associated costs. The author earns money from the royalties of the book sales.

If the book requires an illustrator the publisher will find one that they feel is appropriate for the story. The author usually has little say and usually does not see them until the book has been published.

The publisher takes all of the risk and covers all of the costs. Sometimes publishers enter books in competitions such as the NSW Premier's Literary Awards, Australian Book Industry Awards or The Children's Book Council of Australia Book of the Year Award. These competitions usually have an entry fee which is covered by the publisher.

Tick the boxes and indicate your preference.

☐ Independent/Small Press publishing

Small, independent publishing companies are also traditional publishers. They all have the same roles and responsibilities that have been mentioned above. They are however, small, more intimate companies, with a small staff enabling them to have a closer relationship with the author. Some small companies are boutique publishers, with a specific focus in one area such as children's picture books, or self-help books.

Sometimes, but not always, small, independent publishers will want authors to help promote their own books and may ask for a contribution for competition entry fees.

Beware any publisher who wants to charge you money to publish your book. They are scammers! Publishers never ask for a fee to publish a book.

Self-publishing

☐ Just as the name suggests, this means that you publish your own work. It means that you take all of the responsibility every step of the way, from beginning to end. This includes writing, editing, finding an illustrator if you need one, finding retailers, distributing, promoting and selling your book. There are also legal requirements you have to follow such as getting an ISBN number. ISBN stands for International Standard Book Number and identifies a book and it's edition.

You, as publisher, take all of the responsibility, but this also gives you all of the control to create a product that is in line with your vision.

You own all of the rights which means you get all of the royalties. It also means that you take all of the risk because you are paying for everything from editing, layout, illustrations, printing, distribution and advertising.

Partner Publishing

☐ In Partner Publishing the publisher and author work closely together to produce the book. The publisher and author have different responsibilities, but they both have a shared vision for the book.

The author maintains control of their content and benefits from the expertise and knowledge of the publisher along with having the publisher's endorsement. The publisher benefits because they do not take all of the responsibilty for the costs associated with production and printing.

Literary Agents

☐ The role of an agent is to represent you and your story to a publisher. Because they have worked with publishers they know which stories various publishers would be interested in. Agents also do a lot of the hard work and weed out the weaker manuscripts which means they take the best work to the publishers. The relationship that forms between the author and agent is very important. Agents 'get you', they have your back, they are on your side, they want the best for you.

An agent will have a vision for your manuscript and may make suggestions and tweaks to help it get in the best shape to go before a publisher.

They help to negotiate the contract. They take a fee for their work by taking a percentage of the sales, which this is written into the contract.

Getting an agent can be a challenge but when you have one, they can help your career to bloom.

Write a list of publishers you know. What types of books do they publish? Go to the book stores or library and look for publisher's names. Write them down and record what they publish. i.e picture books, chapter books, self help, biographies etc.

Other ways to be published

There are other ways of being published. These include submitting work to **anthologies**, and **newsletters** produced by Writer's Centres. **Magazines** such as The School Magazine also publish short pieces. Entering competitions is also another option. Apart from being published, **competitions** often have prizes such as manuscript appraisal, access to a publisher, and sometimes a grant to support you to develop your story and career.

These options provide a great way to:
- Start small and build up to more substantial work
- Hone your skills
- Practice at submitting work
- Gain exposure
- Include successful publications on your resume

A little bit about contracts

Contracts are a legal agreement between the author and the publisher. They vary from publisher to publisher and include all sorts of things such as who owns the copyright, and how much the author, illustrator, agent and distributor earn from book sales. These are known as royalties. A large portion of the royalties goes to the publisher because they take all of the risk.

The publisher usually gives an advance to the author and illustrator when the contract is signed. The advance acts as a wage while they work on the story. The amount varies from publisher to publisher. The author does not make any more money on sales until the amount of the advance has been reached. Only then do they receive royalties. So, if a book sells squillions of copies the author will get a lot of royalties. It is common that authors do not make a lot of money from one book. In some contracts, if the book sells poorly and does not reach the advance, the author has to pay the difference back to the publisher.

It is highly recommended that you have a specialist, such as a lawyer look over a contract before you sign it. Or, if you have an agent they will navigate the contract on your behalf. But remember, they also get a percentage of the book sales which means you get less. But, as stated previously they work hard on your behalf to represent you to publishers and help you to reach your goals.

Manuscript submissions

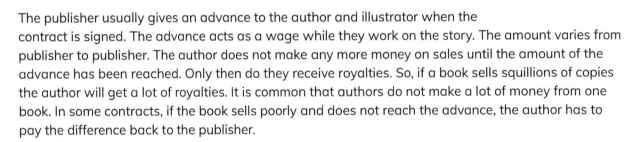

Solicited manuscript
This is when you have an invitation to submit your manuscript to a publisher. This includes a publisher opening submissions on their website, or, if you are at a pitch event, a publisher asking you to email them your manuscript.

Unsolicited manuscript
This is when publishers do not invite you to submit work but you send them your manuscript. When a manuscript goes to a publisher it joins a pile of manuscripts to be read. This is often referred to as the **slush pile**. Publishers can receive hundreds of manuscripts and it can take some time for them to get to yours.

Keeping Track

It is important to keep track of who you contact

Here's Something to help!

It is important to keep track of who you have talked and pitched to. Write down the feedback you recieved and take some time to reflect on it. Even when a pitch has not been successful you often get feedback that is useful. It is important to think about the action you are going to take based on that feedback. Remember, learning and growing is also a measure of your success!

Story submitted: _____

Pitched to: _____

Job title: _____

Company: _____

Contact details: _____

Method of contact (email/face to face): _____ Date_____

Feedback: _____

_____

_____

_____

How will you respond to feedback?: _____
i.e. submit synopsis & manuscript, edit, re-work for a different audience, create a website...

_____

_____

_____

Genre

Genre is the style or category a story is written in

What genre interests you?

Writing in a specific genre creates an expectation for the reader. For instance, if someone wants to be scared, they will read a horror story, if they want to laugh, they will read a comedy. As an author, you need to meet the expectations of your readers.

A publisher will also want to know what genre, or category, you write in. It helps them to promote your book and also helps them to know where it would sit in a bookstore. Even online it will be listed with similar books. Libraries categorise their books by genre too. People often read a specific genre and by keeping them together, whether in a bookstore, online or in a library, readers will know where to find them.

☐ Fiction - made up   ☐ Non-Fiction - not made up

☐ **Action**
As the title suggests, action stories are full of action! They are usually fast paced high pressure situations with characters being hurled from one action scene to the next. This might include scenes involving fighting, chasing, running, escaping. Can you think of more?

☐ **Science Fiction**
Science fiction stories use elements of made up science and technology. They can be set in our world or other worlds and universes with characters that could be human, machine, alien, a combination of these, or completely imaginary creations.

☐ **Fantasy**
Fantasy uses elements of magic and magical creatures to create an imaginary world. Elements include things like enchanted objects such as swords and talismans, dragons, wizards and witches, and spells. Their worlds often include settings such as castles and enchanted forests and weave in prophecy and legend.

} These are known as speculative fiction

☐ **Romance**
The story weaves around the romantic relationship between the main characters.

☐ **Western**
These stories are typically set in the 'Old West' in America and involve characters such as cowboys and Indians, outlaws, sheriffs and pioneers. They are marked by a lawless country, often about rough and tumble people and landscapes such as ranches and small towns that centre around saloons, the bank and the farrier.

☐ **Crime**
In this genre the story revolves around a crime which can include things such as a murder, attack, or even kidnapping . There are usually twists and turns and a series of clues until the guilty person is revealed.

☐ **Horror**
Getting a fright or being terrified is what horror stories aim to do. They often use violence, supernatural elements or blood and gore to scare, shock or disgust the reader.

☐ **Thriller**
Thrillers are the types of stories that keep you on the edge of your seat. They create apprehension, tension, and sometimes a sense of foreboding.

☐ **Biography**
These are stories about real people and tell the story of their life and the things they have experienced. They are often about people who are famous or well known such as athletes, politicians, actors, singers and people who may have done extraordinary things. A similar situation occurs when someone writes their own story, this is called a memoir or an autobiography.

☐ **Academic**
Academic writing is when lecturers at universities write papers that are printed in academic literature such as science magazines. They are analytical and factual and are based on research.

A special word about poetry

☐ **Poetry**
All of these genres can be used when writing poetry. Poetry uses imagery and the sounds of words to create pictures and express ideas and feelings.

> Sometimes you can write in more than one genre. For instance you might write a romance set in a western, or, your story might revolve around a crime that is set in a fantasy world. You could even write an action thriller or a romantic comedy!

Reading helps!

By reading books in a specific genre you begin to understand what your audience enjoys and what will appeal to them. If you have a specific audience it will help you to recognise the language and words that are appropriate for that group. Other useful things you will learn are how to set the story's pace, and how to use dialogue to move a story along. Finding out how authors start and end their stories is useful to understand. Reading will also help you with skills such as the use of punctuation and sentence length (you don't want sentences to be too long or your reader may get lost!). There are many more things you learn by osmosis when you are reading.

Sometimes people worry that by reading other author's books they will accidentally copy them and they won't be able to write anything original. Reading profusely is actually very helpful because it helps you to understand the genre and develop story telling skills.

Get to know your genre

Make a list of books you have read in the genre you will be writing in:

Reading books in this genre will help you understand all the elements specific to that genre. This will help you to write you[r]

_____

_____

_____

_____

_____

_____

Archetypes

Stories use what are called archetypes. Archetypes are elements or traits that are recognisable and universal. For example, when you think of a hero you immediately think of brave, strong and noble.

What are some archetypes in your story? _____

_____

Protagonist

The protagonist is the main character in your story.

As a writer you want readers to identify and empathise with your protagonist, to believe in them, be on their side, wanting them to succeed. Being interested in the protagonist means readers will keep reading to find out what happens to them.

The more you understand your character, what makes them tick, what they like and don't like, and what motivates them, the more you will be able to use these to shape your story. Knowing your characters intimately actually lets you plot your story because you know how they'll interact with the different obstacles thrown at them.

Key things to ask yourself when starting your story are:

- Why is the story worth telling?
  What makes your story interesting or different? Is it the characters, the setting, the plot? Why would someone want to read it?

- What problem faces the protagonist?
  Without a problem there is nothing driving the protagonist's motives. Problems are often referred to as conflict. This does not mean there is fighting, it refers to the different challenges they face. This could be internal: within the character or external: from other people or the environment.

- What motivates the character's actions?
  In other words, why do they react? What are they trying to do, solve, be?

- What traits or archetypes does your protagonist possess?

- What challenges or blocks does your protagonist face? What does your protagonist have to overcome? Challenges and blocks add tension to the story and help to develop your character. These could be generated by other people on purpose or accidentally, the environment such as mountains or distance, the character's own self-doubt, their size, perhaps they are too small or too big to do something they want to do. Conflict, hurdles and challenges can be created by all kinds of things!

Draw your protagonist here:

_____

_____

_____

_____

_____

_____

_____

_____

_____

_____

_____

_____

Picture books

Picture books are traditionally 500 words or less and the illustrations are used to help tell the story. Some are hard covered and some are soft covered. They vary in size and number of pages. These decisions are made by the publisher. If you are writing a picture book, visit your library or local bookshop to get a sense of how they are designed.

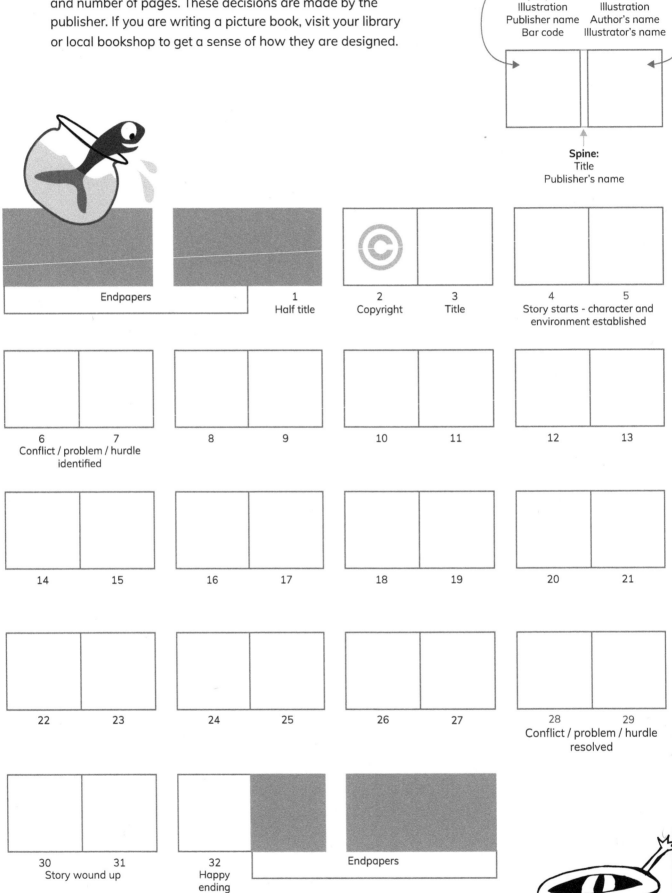

Book covers
Book covers are printed separately on sturdy material to protect the book. They are printed using **hard covers** or **soft covers**. Hard covers are known as the **case** of the book and are attached to the internal pages of the book by end pages. Soft covers do not need end pages. If the book does not have a lot of pages, the inside front cover will be used to contain information about the publisher along with copyright information.

End pages
Hard cover books start and end with end pages. They are used on hard cover books and attach the pages of the book to the book cover with glue. They usually include illustrations and images that are in the story and set the tone of the book. They are like a pause before the story starts.

Half title
This is the very first page of the book and contains just the title of the book.

Copyright
This page contains copyright information about the book such as who owns the text, and illustrations along with the publisher's information and date of publication.

Title
The title page contains the title, subtitle, author, illustrator, publisher and edition.

Pages
Together, the pages in a book are known as the **book block**, the individual pages are referred to as the **leaves**. Books are printed in multiples of 4 which means picture books can vary from 16, 20, 24, 28 or 32 pages.

Not all books have separate half title, copyright or title pages, and some may be combined, but this template will give you some ideas about what to expect if you are creating a picture book. Cost of production will influence the number of pages and production quality of a book. These decisions are made by the publisher.

A template helps with planning. The illustrator usually decides how the text is broken up and where it lives on each page. It is useful for authors to understand this process, especially if you want to be an author/illustrator.

Illustrators add rough sketches to the template to indicate and plan what happens on each page. This is then cut up and put together and becomes what is known as a dummy book. It is a mock-up of the book and captures what it will look like when it is finished. Once this is approved the illustrator begins work on the final illustrations.

Audience
To sell a book you need to know who will read it

who is your story aimed at?

Knowing your audience means you write about things that interest that particular group and in a way that is appropriate for them. It means that booksellers can promote your book to the right group and that audiences can also locate it easier.

☐ **0 - Toddlers**
These are sturdy, thick cardboard or plastic books that have limited or no text and use simple imagery. They focus on things such as colours, numbers, objects, plants and animals. For example, "A is for apple, the ball is blue, the duck is yellow, the cow goes moo."

☐ **Picture Books**
4-8 year olds
Picture books use a combination of illustrations and text to tell the story. The illustrations often expand the story or create a sub-story. Themes are varied and cover many topics from family, friends, environments and feelings. Because they are for children who do not yet read, they are designed to be read out loud by an adult such as a parent, grandparent or teacher. This means that the adult is there to guide them, point things out, and talk to them about the story as they go. Topics vary widely from things they know, and things they will not have encountered. They include stories about family, friends, the environment, and all kinds of things. Having an adult present means that the stories can also focus on more serious themes such as death, or old age because the adult is there to help the child navigate concepts and emotions.

☐ **Teenagers**
Many teenagers still love picture books and you will find some are specifically aimed at them. They provide opportunities for readers of all reading levels to engage in the story, and explore themes at a deeper level. Picture books invite readers to consider a wide variety of meanings and allow for different interpretations. This makes them a good choice for robust, stimulating discussion where ideas and themes can be teased out and unpacked, especially as high school English texts. Themes can touch on more sensitive issues such as loss and grief, resilience, war, loneliness, love and relationships and provide opportunities for self-reflection.

Tick the boxes and indicate your preference.

Chapter books
6-9 year olds

These are written for newly independent readers. Chapters are short and manageable so that readers have a sense of achievement. The language is simple, using short sentences. Multiple illustrations help tell the story and keep the book visually fun and interesting. The number of words per book vary between publishers. Children of this age, early level readers, are still very much surrounded by family and friends so themes tend to revolve around this.

9-12 year olds

This age group, known as middle-grade, are more confident readers so chapters are longer with fewer illustrations. Themes reflect their own exploration and desire for independence from family so they often involve adventures with friends out in the world. However, they always have the backdrop of family security and safety to return to.

Young Adult
This is the 12-18 age group

The chapters are longer with no illustrations, although, sometimes decorative features are used on chapter headings. They are written in a wide variety of genres. The feature that distinguishes them from adult fiction is the age of the protagonist and other characters. While ages of characters can vary, the main characters need to be teenagers. The age of the teenager indicates whether it is aimed at the lower or upper end of that age range. Stories center on issues that interest teenagers such as independence and the transition from childhood to adulthood but sex is taboo. The story may involve romance, but it is never explicit.

Adult
This encompasses the 18+ age group

The characters can be of any age but the tone of the story is distinctly adult and the way it is told is more complex. Genre varies widely and topics can be explored more deeply in a more explicit manner.

Young readers like to read about characters that are slightly older than themselves. 7 year olds will want to read about 10 year olds, 11 year olds will want to read about 13 year olds.

Take this into account when considering your audience. This will affect the language you choose, complexity of sentences, number of words as well as the themes you tackle.

Community

Finding your 'people' can support your success

How can a posse help you?

Building a community of like minded people will help you learn more about the industry, how other people work and you can use this information to influence your writing practice. Community provides support and friendship and understanding because they 'get it'. It can be scary sharing your work with others so you need to find people you trust. You want them to be encouraging but not to inflate your ego. Honest but not brutal.

☐ ### Writers' Centres
Check out your national, state and local writers' centres. They are a wealth of information about publishing, copyright and contracts. They offer newsletters, workshops and support and promote authors and illustrators. Not only do they help build a sense of community, some advocate and protect the rights of authors and illustrators and keep members up to date with changes that impact the industry.

☐ ### Workshops
Not only will you be able to learn from the experienced facilitators, it is a great way to meet like-minded people. Facilitators share their unique knowledge and processes. By going to a variety of workshops you will be able to integrate what you learn and develop your own ways of doing things. Use opportunities such as workshops to connect with facilitators and participants and support one another as you develop your career. Writers are a very friendly bunch and are often willing to share valuable experience.

I encourage you to attend workshops even if they may not always appear relevant. Author facilitators are very generous, they often give you useful information about how to approach publishers. Or, information about other aspects of writing you may not have considered. For instance. I once attended a fantasy fiction workshop where the facilitator not only talked about magical elements, they talked about the voice of the character. This included vocabulary and tone, and how this determines not only the age of the character but the age of the reader. This information could be applied to any genre. So, in short, don't make assumptions or limit yourself. Put yourself in a position to learn as much as you can from different sources.

☐ ### Writers' festivals
Writers' festivals are a great way to find out about authors and how they have succeeded. No two authors will be the same. Use this information and integrate it to inform your own decisions. You will also meet lots of like-minded audience participants so it is a great opportunity to make connections and form friendships. Some festivals provide workshops and opportunities to pitch manuscript ideas so learn as much as you can and make the most of it!

☐ ## Mentors
Mentoring is a formal relationship between a mentor, someone who has knowledge and expertise in a specific area, and the mentee, the person who is being nurtured. The mentor acts as a guide and advisor to help the mentee reach their goals over a specified time.

☐ ## Agents
An agent is a marvelous form of support. Not only do they represent your work to publishers, they have your back. They are encouraging, supportive and offer advice. Agents are the buffer between you and the publisher. They are your personal cheer squad, and can help motivate you, stroke a bruised ego and negotiate contracts on your behalf. This is a formal relationship and the agent receives a percentage of the book sales as stated in the contract.

☐ ## Online groups
Online groups such as the ones you find on social media can be a great way to connect with other creative people. Sharing and seeing what they are doing can help you to feel that you are part of a community of like-minded people. They don't all have to be writers, they can be other creative industries such as painters, ceramicists, and musicians. They all understand the drive to be creative and often share their creative practice.

☐ ## Family and friends
Family and friends are wonderful supporters. They will encourage you unconditionally, but remember, they may have limited knowledge about writing and their bias may mean they think everything you do is marvellous. So, use them as a support but seek feedback from professionals, such as editors, if you want critical feedback.

> Learn from everyone but find your own way. Find what works for you. Go to workshops and talks, watch video interviews. Participate and talk in formal and informal settings. Learn as much as you can from others, then shuffle, sieve, absorb and integrate everything you have learnt. Let this knowledge blend and inform your practice and find a way of working that suits you best.

Motivation
Motivation will keep you going

How much do you want 'it'?

How much you want to be an author and get your story into the world will influence your motivation, perseverance, and determination to succeed. This is particularly important during times when you might not be having the success you would like. Sometimes you can wait a long time to hear from a publisher after you have pitched a book idea. Sometimes, even when you are successful it can be a long time, even years, before your book is ready for sale. Being determined and tenacious will help you to not give up, even when you might feel like it.

Where are you on the **motivation thermometer?**

Absolutely driven!
I won't stop until I succeed!

Maybe
It is a nice idea, maybe someday...

Are you happy where you sit on your thermometer or would you like it to change?

☐ **No! It's perfect**
Wacko, keep going!

☐ **Yes! I want to change this.**
You need to do things that will ignite your motivation. This could include talking with a creative friend, mentor, or getting inspiration from attending a workshop.

Write down some things that will help motivate you. Break it down, small steps are easier to achieve:

_____

_____

_____

Voice

Voice sets the tone and mood of a story

What makes the way you communicate unique?

The voice of a writer refers to the style in which they write. The only way to find your style is to write, write, and write! The more you write the more your authentic, individual and unique voice will emerge. No one else is you, no one else has had your life with your experiences, only you can write like you.

The voice develops naturally in the way that an author expresses themselves. Every book reflects a tone, or the voice of the author. This can be positive or negative, playful or serious, formal or informal, irreverent or respectful, all manner of things. For instance, the tone of this book is playful. The evidence for this? The casual comments, advice and sharing of personal experiences in a conversational manner. The illustrations also bring a fun, uplifting, friendly tone to the book. Together, all of these things set the tone and mood of this book. They reflect my feelings and attitude to the topic. I wanted to demonstrate that you do not have to be too serious, that you have permission to play and have fun while you pursue your goals.

An audience not only connects with a story because of its subject matter, but by how it is told. They are listening to the voice of the author whether they realize it or not. Authors can use this to their advantage when targeting a specific audience. For instance, chapter books that use first person narrators who talk directly to the reader. They are using this tone, style, voice, to directly connect with the audience, on their level.

Your voice will develop naturally. So, just play, have fun, be experimental and eventually a natural way of expressing yourself will develop. Another way to build your awareness of voice is to read widely. When reading, take a moment to identify the tone or mood of the book. How would you describe the voice of the book to someone?

1 _____
_____
_____

2 _____
_____
_____
_____

Think about the last two books you have read. How would you describe the voice? What made it unique?

Willingness

Being open to suggestions and compromising is part of the process

How willing are you?

An aspect of writing that is not often considered is how willing you are to work at your success. It takes effort to succeed. It takes commitment and an investment of your time and energy. Then, if you are successful at gaining a publisher you need to consider how willing you are to work with them. Just like you, they will have a vision for your book and this may mean they want to change or reshape certain aspects of it in order to meet that vision.

☐ **Have you got more?**
Is your story a one off or do you have more ideas? If you are successful your publisher will want to build on that success. Do you have more stories in you and is that something you want to pursue?

☐ **Write, write and write**
To get better at anything you need to practice. Writing is the same, to get better you need to put in effort and time. This means you need to write, write, and keep on writing!

Be easy to work with so that the publisher wants to work with you again!

☐ **Persevere**
Submitting a manuscript also brings rejection. It can be hard to keep going and continue to submit to new publishers knowing that they too might not want to publish your book. Rejection of a manuscript can feel personal and you do not always know why it is rejected because they give very little, if any, feedback. It can be disheartening so you need to be resilient and you need to rally yourself and be willing to keep going!

You don't want to be a pushover, but you also don't want to be difficult to work with.

☐ **Make changes**
Before your story is edited a publisher may want you to change something about your story. For instance they may want you to reduce the words, or, they may suggest that it be aimed at a younger audience which means you have to simplify the words and re-write scenes. They may even want to change a character so that the story will appeal to a broader audience. Authors can feel very protective about their work so you need to think about how open you will be if requests like this are made. It may surprise you, but the changes often make a stronger story. You need to know when to stand your ground and when to yield. If you are too rigid your story may not progress to being published so you need to ask yourself what you are willing to negotiate and compromise over.

Creating a great working relationship is fun for them and fun for you!

☐ Let an editor amend your work

Once your manuscript is accepted the publisher will give it to an editor for proofing. They may make changes such as replacing words, deleting text, or suggest alternative text. They sometimes suggest big structural changes or altering characters. This is a natural part of the publishing process, but how willing are you to accept these changes or compromise?

☐ No way, it's perfect the way it is!
This might jeopardise your contract. However, if maintaining total control is important to you then consider self-publishing.

☐ Yes, I am willing to compromise.
I am open to working with the publisher and making changes.

☐ Illustrations

If you have written a picture book the publisher usually chooses an illustrator. This means that you have no say in the style of illustrations and you do not see them until the book is finished. Well-known authors have more autonomy about the illustration style, but unknown authors do not, especially at larger publishing companies. You may have more involvement with a small independent publisher.

☐ Discipline

Sometimes you are not in the mood to write but, there is no way around it, you simply have to get the manuscript finished. Sometimes, there will be all sorts of distractions both real and imagined and plenty of things to help you procrastinate. You need strength of character to wrangle yourself and make yourself do it. The biggest commitment you have made is to yourself, so, are you willing to do what it takes when you would rather be sitting in the sun having cups of tea and chatting to a friend? Are you determined to finish your manuscript? You need to ask yourself if you can be disciplined.

☐ Sacrifice

It takes grit and determination to reach goals when you would rather be doing other things like having fun with family and friends. But the manuscript won't write itself and sometimes you just have to miss out. But, rest assured, once it is done you will reap the rewards of your sacrifices and you can feel proud of your achievement. But, you need to ask yourself, is the sacrifice worth it?

A publisher may want to change all sorts of things from a characters name, or gender or make your main character an animal rather than a person. They could even ask you to turn a chapter book into a picture book.

Developing your story becomes a collaboration!

Start!

You have to start somewhere so just start

Are you ready to start?

Starting is sometimes the hardest thing to do. There is no such thing as the right time, the right mood, the right working conditions. It does not matter if the house is clean or messy, if the kids are in bed, you are on holiday, or about to retire. JUST START! No one is going to pluck your idea out of your head! Just start, write a few words, then a sentence, then a paragraph, then a page, then a chapter… and keep going!

Once you start, remember, it doesn't have to be good. The beginning is just for you. Just get it out of your head and onto paper or into the computer. Editing, crafting and polishing can come later. You don't have to share it with anyone at this point. If that inner critic pops up in your head just tell it to calm down and give you the space to enjoy yourself. Life is hard enough without giving ourselves a hard time too!

Don't know what to write? It doesn't matter, just start. Start by describing the things around you, your mood, what the pen feels like in your hand. Then widen it; what are the sounds in the next room, then outside? Then bring something new in, maybe someone comes into the room, who are they? What do they want?

Finish!

Finishing is as important as starting

Are you committed to finishing?

Your manuscript does not have to be perfect, but it does need to be finished in order to get published. So, just finish it! Once it concludes with those fabulous words 'the end' you are free to tweak, start a second draft, or give it to an editor. But, if you are re-working it, remember, you have to finish that too! Again, just finish it!

There are all sorts of reasons people do not finish writing their book; time, writer's block, self-doubt. Whatever your reason, acknowledge it and keep going. Keep going until it is done. Set a goal, or a self-imposed deadline, get it ready for a publisher's submission date or a pitch event, whatever works for you. Set boundaries with your family and friends, let them know how important it is to you and ask them to find ways they can support you. Re-read the section on willingness, in particular, discipline and sacrifice. You have it in you, you've got this!

Submit!

If you don't submit you will never be seen

Can you follow instructions?

No publisher is going to somehow magically find your book and publish it! To be published they need to lay eyes on it and read it! Do you want it to stay in the bottom drawer or in a lonely folder on your computer forever? Do you want to deny future fans the pleasure of reading it? It is only going to go somewhere if you send it out into the world.

Polish your manuscript carefully. Make it as good as possible, but don't be held up by waiting for it to be perfect because it may never be perfect. So, just do it, let go, what's the worst that can happen? It might not be right for one publisher, but it could be just what another publisher is looking for. So, go ahead, you got this, submit!

But, before you hit that submit button, do some research and find the right publisher for your story. Make sure you understand what they are looking for. ONLY send it to publishers who are looking for your type of book.

Read and re-read the submission instructions and follow them. **Follow them EXACTLY!** The next job you have to do is wait. Wait and **be patient.** It can take weeks or months to receive a response. So, in the meantime, get working on something else. It will take your mind off waiting and help you to hone your skills. It also means you have something else ready if they want to see more of your work.

Apart from submitting your manuscript, (or in some cases just the first chapter), you will also need a synopsis and a cover letter.

- [ ] ## Synopsis
  This includes the type of book it is, (chapter, picture book etc), genre, word count and the target audience. It provides a brief summary of the story, plot (including the ending) and characters. Keep it clear and concise.

- [ ] ## Cover letter
  This involves introducing yourself and your manuscript to the publisher. Include your writing history such as previous publications, any competitions you may have been placed in, and your qualifications. Include what makes you knowledgeable in this area i.e. what makes you the best person to write this story?

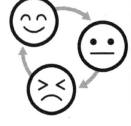

Highs and Lows

The emotional range of an author can be surprising

How will you manage your emotions?

The emotions you will experience when setting out to become a published author may surprise you. It certainly surprised me! Being honest with yourself and acknowledging your emotions is extremely important for mental health and resilience. Having a supportive posse behind you is so important. They will be there through the highs and lows and help you to maintain balance, perspective and sanity! Also, listen. Listen to others, acknowledge their feelings and build a supportive network. Talking and sharing helps!

Where are you on the this wheel?

Understanding your emotions is an important aspect of maintaining a healthy mindset. Allow them to be there. It is ok to feel overwhelmed or deflated from time to time. It is equally ok to delight and take pride in your achievements.

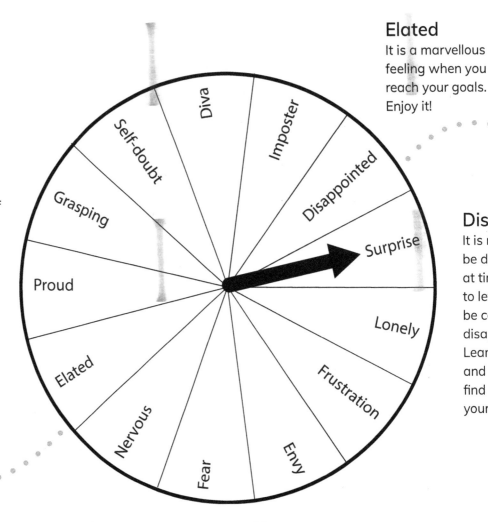

Elated
It is a marvellous feeling when you reach your goals. Enjoy it!

Disappointed
It is natural to be disappointed at times. Try not to let yourself be consumed by disappointment. Lean on your family and friends and find ways to lift your spirits.

Lonely
People often have a romantic notion about writers. But, the reality is, you are working alone, often for long periods of time. It can be an isolating profession. Your posse are an important support network that will help to keep you connected to people.

Nervous
Nerves can flare up when you are pitching to publishers. Try to be as organised as possible. Practice your pitch, practice it a lot. Remember, they want you to succeed. They want to find a winner, so, take a breath and steady yourself.

Divas
Are you offended and aghast at the thought of making changes to your manuscript? Are you interpreting constructive feedback as negative or insulted by it? You might be being a diva! Take a step back. You might want to step off your high horse and change your perspective. Think about what you can learn. Divas are hard to work with. No one wants to work with difficult people.

Nervous
Sharing manuscripts and submitting and pitching can really peak nervousness and anxiety.

Surprise
Opportunities will come along that you do not expect. For example, I was delightfully surprised when a local TV station found out about my first book and interviewed me. I was on the 6:30 news that night! Enjoy the surprises!

Fear
Fear can be paralyzing. Fear of looking stupid, fear of failing, even fear of success can stop us from achieving our goals. Do not let it be a block to your success.

Proud
Quite simply, be proud of your achievements!

Envy
It is natural to feel envious when others succeed where we don't. But, sometimes, others will be jealous of **you**! This may put you in an awkward position, you may even feel guilty, but remember, it is their envy, and they are responsible for it, not you. Own your success. And, if you feel envy rising in you try to turn it around, take the focus off you, celebrate and rejoice in other's success, it may feel fake and uncomfortable at first, but practice, delight in people's success, it will make you feel better and cultivate an abundance mentality. There really is enough success for everyone!

Self-doubt
Sometimes self-doubt will sabotage success. You might even be given an opportunity to submit a manuscript but don't due to self doubt. Never miss out on an opportunity because of it.

Imposter syndrome
Just own it, you ARE a writer. Use language that positively frames who you are as an author, now, in this moment. There are always going to be people who are better and more successful, or worse and less successful than you. You are you, no one else has your experiences, no one else is going to write like you. Eventually the uncomfotable feeling will wear off.

Frustration
It can be a frustrating industry. Everything takes so long, find ways to deal with your frustration, cultivate patience or, if that doesn't work, go break a few plates in the backyard! But, don't stop, never stop, just keep going. Have several projects on the go so you can flick between them, stay connected to your writing. Remind yourself regularly what you love about it.

Grasping
Beware the grasping of others. Even a small amount of success will see others interrogating you to find out how you did it. They want a short cut, they want to replicate that success for themselves. But each person's success is unique, and everyone has to find their own way of doing things. My advice here is to point them in the direction of a writers' centre where they can find out about workshops. Re-read the section in this book about community and suggest these to them. Likewise, try not to grasp at other's success. Show gratitude and learn in many different ways such as speaking events, workshops, social media comments. Then integrate it and find your own way to success.

Feedback
Feedback will help you to grow

Can you put your ego aside?

Feedback is an important part of growth as a writer. It can be scary showing someone your work. You can feel vulnerable. Even if you do not receive the feedback you were hoping for, don't lose hope. You might be offended, or deflated. You might want to give up. But, if you put your ego aside and be objective, then you will get better as a writer.

Do you really want it?
Think carefully before you ask someone for feedback. What is your motivation? Do you really want to know what they think or do you want them to like your story no matter what? It is easy to take feedback as negative criticism but critical feedback can be a very quick and powerful way to learn and improve. Treat feedback as a gift, a gift that informs your writing and career.

Be prepared to **listen**. You do not have to agree with all critical feedback, there is always give and take. It might be appropriate to disagree and clarify your intentions, but don't ever, under any circumstances argue. It is just rude. It is uncomfortable for them and uncomfortable for you. You also risk coming across as a bit of a diva. People tend to avoid divas. **Say thank you**. If you find yourself taking offence, take a moment and try to listen without reacting. There could be some truth that would actually improve your manuscript. Try their suggestions, you have nothing to lose. If it works great, if not, then you have lost nothing.

Some people will not want to give feedback because they have been stung before. Respect their choice to refrain and go to a professional. There are editors and author/editors who provide feedback and guidance as part of their business. There will be a fee but it will be worth it.

Beware of friends and family, while they are supportive and most likely have nothing but praise to give, they usually have limited knowledge about crafting a manuscript and about what publishers are looking for. So, while they are great for your morale, they may not have the skills that will help polish your work.

Types of feedback
The types of feedback you receive can be surprising to new writers. You might even get conflicting feedback from different people. Feedback can include all kinds of things such as *the manuscript is too long, too complicated, nothing happens, make the characters animals, the language does not match the age of your intended audience, or, the sentences are too long*. Feedback covers a vast range of things. You will get more comfortable receiving feedback as your experience and confidence grows.

> Feedback is worthless unless you do something with it. So, take it onboard, filter and digest it. What ACTION will you now take?

Vision

Being clear about what you want will help you to achieve it

What does your future look like?

A vision is about creating a dream or a purpose. It is something that you imagine for yourself so that you can work towards it. You can write your vision as a sentence, or as a collection of words. You can draw it or create a moodboard to put on your wall or save electronically. However you choose to create your vision, put it where you can see it so that you are regularly reminded of your goals.

Write your goals here and describe what success looks like. Include drawings and photos that inspire you!

A Quick Review!

PLAY

Don't take yourself too seriously. Being too serious or tight can stifle the life from your work. Explore, write, doodle, have fun, but write something, anything! Sometimes these playful works can lead to ideas that you can use and refine. This is just for you, no one else, it does not matter how good these are.

POSEE

Create a supportive community of like-minded people around you who you can learn from and trust. Who will support you when you are struggling, and who will celebrate your successes with you?

LEARN

Attend workshops, talks, events, anything you can, to learn from others. Even if they are not quite the area you want to write in, attend because there are other things you will learn that will inform your writing. You willl also find out valuable information about the publishing industry.

EASY

Be easy to work with so publishers want to work with you. You will have to make compromises and changes to your manuscript along the way. This is a natural part of the collaboration process.

AGE

You are NEVER too old. I was 53 when I had my first book published. I have a friend who just turned 74 and his first book will be launched this year!

SUBMIT

When submitting a manuscript follow the submissions guidelines exactly!

CELEBRATE

Celebrating achievements is really important. Every success, no matter how small, is a step forward. Every step along the way is worth celebrating.

GRATITUDE

Appreciate those who share their knowledge with you. Their experience has been hard earned, they have worked hard for their success. Every bit of advice, knowledge or technique they share informs you and helps you to move closer to your goals. Be generous in return.

FEELINGS

You will feel deflated from time to time, progress can be slow and it can feel as though there are a lot of hurdles in your way. Remember, all emotions are temporary, and successes, no matter how small, will also come your way. Find ways to feed your soul during tough times.

SUBMERGE

Read, read, read. Find books you like and pay attention to what you like about them. What draws you to keep reading? What genre is it, who is the protagonist, what archetypes are used? Being aware of these things will help you to bring clarity and direction to your work.

VOICE

Everyone has a way of expressing themselves that is unique to them. To find your voice write, write, write and your style will emerge.

FEEDBACK

Constructive feedback helps you grow. Put your ego aside and try to look at it objectively. It does not mean you have to agree with all feedback, but, accept it, and say thank you.

CPSIA information can be obtained
at www.ICGtesting.com
Printed in the USA
LVHW071210040421
683394LV00013B/1628